I Got a Pet!

My Pet Dog

By Brienna Rossiter

www.littlebluehousebooks.com

Little Blue House is distributed by North Star Editions:
sales@northstareditions.com | 888-417-0195

Produced for Little Blue House by Red Line Editorial.

Photographs ©: Shutterstock Images, cover, 4, 7, 9, 13 (top), 13 (bottom), 14–15, 16, 19, 21, 23 (top), 24 (top left), 24 (top right), 24 (bottom right); iStockphoto, 10, 23 (bottom), 24 (bottom left)

Library of Congress Control Number: 2022901950

ISBN
978-1-64619-586-2 (hardcover)
978-1-64619-613-5 (paperback)
978-1-64619-665-4 (ebook pdf)
978-1-64619-640-1 (hosted ebook)

Printed in the United States of America
Mankato, MN
082022

About the Author

Brienna Rossiter is a writer and editor who lives in Minnesota.

Table of Contents

My Pet Dog

I have a dog.

I love my dog.

I pet my dog.

His fur is soft.

fur

I play with my dog.

I throw a ball.

My dog brings it back to me.

ball

shake

Tricks and Training

I teach my dog tricks.

I teach my dog to shake.

I train my dog every day. He learns to sit and lie down.

sit

lie down

I tell my dog to do a trick.

He does what I ask.

I give him a treat.

treat

bowl

Dog Care

I give my dog water
and food.
I put them in bowls.

I take my dog for walks.

I use a leash.

leash

I bring bags on our walks.

I pick up my dog's poop.

I throw it away.

bag

I help my dog stay clean.

I give my dog baths.

I brush my dog's fur.

brush

Glossary

bowls

leash

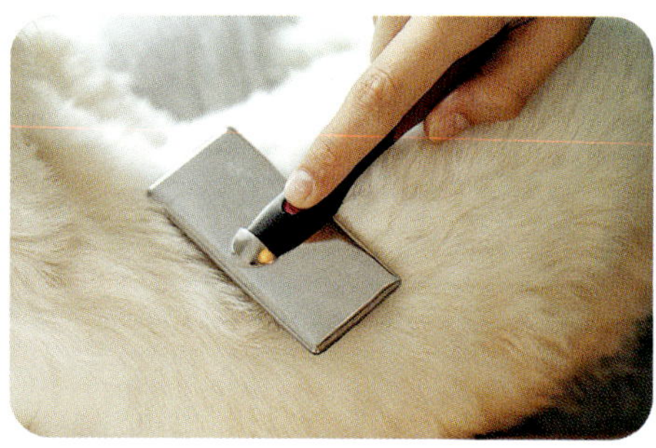

brush

treats

Index